The Christmas Book

by Moira Eastman and Wendy Poussard
design and illustration by Robyn Carter
music by Christopher Willcock

© 1980 Ave Maria Press
Notre Dame, Indiana 46556

How Christmas Began

At Christmas we remember how Jesus came into our world as a tiny baby. Christmas is his birthday, a time for happiness, parties, gifts and songs. All over the world, people look forward to Christmas, and wish each other joy and peace.

No one knows exactly when Jesus was born. If he had been the son of a king or an emperor, his birth would have been carefully recorded, but no one bothered to write down the birthday of a poor baby, born in a stable at Bethlehem, the child of ordinary travellers.

Much later, when Jesus' life on earth was over, people wanted to read his story. Then Matthew, a tax gatherer, and a doctor named Luke each wrote about the first Christmas. This story was told around the world, travelled down the years, and is told again each year at Christmas time.

Matthew and Luke did not know the day or the month of Jesus' birthday. So how was the date of Christmas decided? Long ago, many years before Jesus came, people of the ancient world celebrated, in the cold of winter, "the birthday of the unconquered sun." They ate huge feasts. They decorated their houses with holly, ivy and mistletoe.

Although the sky was gray and the fields were bare, people knew that from this day on the sun would grow stronger and warmer. The Romans kept "the birthday of the unconquered sun" on December 25.

Years passed, and many, many people remembered the story and followed the teaching of Jesus. They too wanted to celebrate a time of hope. They turned the feast of the sun into the feast of Christ's Mass. The sun brought warmth and growth to a winter world. Like the sun, the baby of Bethlehem brought hope to Christian hearts.

From the fifth to the tenth century, Christ's Mass marked the start of the church's year. By the sixth century it was a public holiday. The Roman Emperor Justinian declared that no one was to work on that day. Since then, in every century, every land has had its own Christmas customs and signs. Candles, stars, flowers, stockings, trees, puddings, cookies, holly, reindeer, carols, gifts, a hundred ways of making a Happy Christmas.

Here are some children's ideas about Christmas.

Christmas brings people together.

Christmas is a time to be merry.

Christmas is a great day because it is the birthday of Jesus.

We wish each other a happy Christmas.

Christmas is to me a festive time of friendship and a happy time to spend with our family.

I believe myself that Christmas is a time for unbounded joy.

Christmas to me means presents, food and fun. Everyone's in a good mood.

When I think of Christmas I think of . . .
Make a list with your family or friends.

The Promised Son

The people of Israel were people of promise. Yahweh, the God of Israel promised that he would watch over and be with his people. The Bible story tells how Israel forgot, over and over again, to keep her part of the promise. Over and over, the people turned to evil ways, putting riches, other gods, their own comfort and pleasure before Yahweh. Always, they brought on themselves disasters of war, disease and poverty. But always Yahweh stayed with them. He sent them holy men, prophets, to warn, teach and guide them back to his paths. And often there were promises of a special one who would be born to save the people. Here are some of the hints the prophets gave about the Promised Son.

A Ruler Born in Bethlehem

The prophet Micah spoke of Bethlehem as the birthplace of the one who is to rule over Israel. This is what he said:

> The Lord says, "Bethlehem . . . you are one of the smallest towns in Judah, but out of you I will bring a ruler for Israel, . . . When he comes he will rule his people with the strength that comes from the Lord and with the majesty of the Lord God himself."
>
> Mi 5: 2, 4

After Jesus died, his friends remembered this prophecy, and realized that even in little ways Jesus filled the description of "the one who is to come."

A Good Shepherd

Ezekiel was one of the prophets. He lived almost 600 years before Jesus was born, at the time when Jerusalem was invaded by the Babylonians. Most of the Israelites were taken to Babylon as slaves. Ezekiel went too. Yahweh sent him messages for the people—warnings to the kings, warnings to the people to change their ways, and promises of his love and care for those who were faithful.

Here is a message from Yahweh that Ezekiel gave the rulers of Israel. He calls the rulers shepherds and the people sheep.

You are doomed, you shepherds of Israel. You take care of yourselves, but never tend the sheep. You drink the milk, wear clothes made from the wool, and kill and eat the finest sheep. . . . But you have not taken care of the weak ones, healed those that are sick, bandaged those that are hurt . . . or looked for those that were lost.

I will take my sheep away from you bad shepherds. . . . I will give them a king like my servant David, to be their one shepherd and he will take care of them.

Ez 34: 2-5, 10, 23

When Jesus came, he called himself "The Good Shepherd." People remembered then the promise from God that Ezekiel had spoken.

When Jesus was born in a stable far from home, it was only shepherds who were told the secret of who he was, and they came to worship and welcome him.

A King Riding on a Donkey

The prophet Zechariah lived about 500 years before the birth of Jesus. Here is part of what he said:

> Shout for joy, you people of Jerusalem!
> Look, your king is coming to you!
> He comes triumphant and victorious,
> but humble and riding on a donkey—
> on a colt, the foal of a donkey.
>
> Zec 9:9

Most Christmas cribs include an ox and a donkey. Perhaps Mary rode that donkey to Bethlehem. Later in Jesus' life he rode a donkey to Jerusalem and the people greeted him as a great king.

A Servant of the Poor

The prophet Isaiah foretold the coming of a servant of God who would be scorned and rejected. By his suffering he would save many men. This is part of what Isaiah said about the "suffering servant."

> He was arrested and sentenced and
> led off to die,
> and no one cared about his fate.
> He was put to death for the sins
> of our people.

> He was placed in a grave with evil men,
> he was buried with the rich,
> even though he had never committed a crime
> or ever told a lie.
>
> Is 53: 8-9

Jesus was born in a stable. There was no room for him in the house. Many of the people of Israel expected their savior to come as a mighty king, but he was born a suffering servant of the poor.

A Family Waits to Be Together

Barbara and Stefan lived in Yugoslavia. They were not rich, but their life was peaceful and happy. The countryside was beautiful, and they did not go hungry or cold. They had three beautiful children, a girl, Mira, then a boy, Marko, and another girl, Katica.

Then the Second World War came, and their whole lives changed. German forces gained control of the part of Yugoslavia where they lived, and the strong men were sent to work for the German army and to work in German factories. Soon Stefan had to go. He had no choice.

Barbara and the children missed him so much. And Stefan was even lonelier because he was away from all his family and in a country with a strange language. They were sad, hard times. There was fighting and bombing all over Europe. Sometimes Barbara and Stefan felt that they would never see each other again.

After two years, when the war was over, Stefan returned home. It was so wonderful to be together again. Their time of separation had taught them how much they loved each other, how good it was just to be together. But their troubles were not over. The new government in Yugoslavia was communist. Stefan and Barbara were Catholics. They went to Mass every Sunday and followed their church's laws and customs. They could see they would never get on well with this government, which did not approve of their religion. Also Stefan wanted to go back to his small carpentry business, but the only work he could get was in a government factory.

At night, when the children had gone to bed, they could hear Stefan and Barbara talking late into the night, trying to work out what to do. At last they decided to make a new life in another part of the world. They worked hard and saved every cent. There were hardly ever any treats or outings for the children. There was no time, and their money was needed to pay Stefan's fare.

One morning, when the children awoke, their father had gone. He did not say goodbye. The government would not allow anyone to leave the country, so he did not tell anyone how or when he was getting away.

Barbara lost her job at the hospital. This was to punish her for Stefan's escape. She did sewing, cleaning and cooking for other women, and she made more plans of her own.

One day Barbara took Mira and Katica to her sister's place and kissed them goodbye. "Don't be afraid," she told them. "You know your father went to America. Now Marko and I are going to follow him. As soon as I get there, I will work too and we will get tickets for you both as soon as we can. It will be a long time, at least two or three years! You will be very sad and miss us a lot. Be patient and remember that it will be worth it all. There will be a good life for us all in America. I will not be able to write, because the government might open the letters. Be patient and strong and don't ever doubt that I will get you out. I will not forget you for a minute. I must hurry now.

Goodbye and God take care of you till we meet again."

There was a big funeral at the next town that day. The man who died had been well known and he had many children, grandchildren and great-grandchildren.

Barbara hurried home, dressed herself and Marko in black funeral clothes, picked a big bunch of flowers and walked to the funeral. Many people had come from villages across the border in Italy. The guards were not too fussy about the villagers travelling back and forth for such events, and Barbara and Marko passed the border without being noticed. And so another time of waiting began.

Every night Barbara and Marko (who were living in a camp for homeless people) talked about Stefan and the girls and wondered about the new land where they were going. Every night Mira and Katica dreamed of the time when they would all be together again and the whole family could spend a wonderful day swimming at a sunny, sandy beach.

Every day Stefan went to work early, and worked overtime whenever he could. Every week he counted his money. He counted how many more weeks it would be till the family was together again.

It seemed a long, long time for all of them before their dream at last came true.

> Have you ever waited for something you wanted very much?

> Have you ever had to trust that someone would not forget you?

Time to Get Ready

Words by WENDY POUSSARD

Music by CHRISTOPHER WILLCOCK

With a clear beat

1. Mo- ses wai- ted in the desert for for- ty years. He
2. Ma- ry wai- ted in the winter for a ba- by boy To
3. We are wai- ting for the kingdom of the Lord to come With the

1. comfor- ted the people and wiped away their tears. But he felt so tired of waiting, Lord.
2. change her life and fill it full of pain and joy. But she felt so tired of waiting, Lord.
3. lion and the lamb lying in the sun. But we feel so tired of waiting, Lord.

1. You know you promised. You gave your word, It's a long, long time of wai- ting.
2. You know you promised. You gave your word, It's a long, long time of wai- ting.
3. You know you promised. You gave your word, It's a long, long time of wai- ting.

Refrain: We are wai-ting, Waiting is slow, Time for dreaming, Time to grow.

Time to get ready be- fore we start. Time to store things in our hearts.

Advent Wreath

An Advent wreath is a circle of greenery with four candles. Each Sunday in Advent, place the wreath on the table and light the candles before the evening meal. One candle is lit on the first Sunday of Advent, two on the second Sunday and so on.

MAKING AN ADVENT WREATH

Make a circle of an evergreen branch. Tie it so that it will hold its shape. Put the wreath on a table and arrange four candle-sticks and candles inside the circle.

OR

Cut a circle from cardboard. Paint or draw green leaves over the circle, or cut leaves from green paper and glue them over the wreath. Place clay candlesticks on the wreath (see page 36 for how to make the candlesticks).

The following verses can be said at the lighting of the Advent candles.

Lighting the Advent Candles

The First Candle

Reader   God sends his bright dawn
to light and to shine
on the people who live
in the darkness.

All   Please God make us strong
in doing your will
making Christ welcome
this time when he comes.

The Second Candle

Reader   Wake up. Wake up.
The night is over.
No time for sleeping,
hiding in the dark.

All   No time for fighting,
hurting and grabbing.
Lord teach us peace
to follow your path.

The Third Candle

Reader   Rain on a desert
turns it to flowers.
Look, God is coming.
Let's open our hearts.

All   Let us feel the joy
his coming will bring.
Lord change our lives
to welcome this king.

The Fourth Candle

Reader   Let us pray now as
Advent is ending
that Christ will truly
come into our hearts.

All   Mary trusted God.
His plans changed her life.
Let's open our lives
to the Spirit of God.

Advent Calendar

Advent means "coming." Before Christmas, the church has a time to wait, prepare and hope for the coming of Jesus at Christmas. This time is called Advent, and it begins four Sundays before Christmas Day.

To make the Advent calendar:

1. Copy these pages. (Permission is given to duplicate the Advent Calendar.) Attach the third and fourth weeks to the first and second weeks.

FIRST SUNDAY IN ADVENT	MONDAY	TUESDAY	WEDNESDAY
BE READY	This week, write a Christmas letter.	*Do not be afraid — I am with you! I am your God — let nothing terrify you!* *Is 41*	Make a pictu or model abo being ready.
SECOND SUNDAY IN ADVENT	MONDAY	TUESDAY	WEDNESDAY
PREPARE	This week, make a Christmas poster.	*Sing a new song to the Lord! Sing to the Lord, all the world!* *Ps 96*	Tell or write a story about preparing. Share your sto with a friend.

2. Make four strips of doors. Attach the strips above each week of the calendar as shown. (See the illustrations on pages 14 and 15.) Each day cut away one door.

THURSDAY	FRIDAY	SATURDAY
Trust in the Lord forever; he will always protect us. *Is 26*	Give away some kind words.	Think quietly for five minutes about the people you love.

THURSDAY	FRIDAY	SATURDAY
The trees in the woods will shout for joy when the Lord comes to rule the earth. *Ps 96*	Give away a smile.	Think quietly for five minutes about the gifts you have given and received in your life.

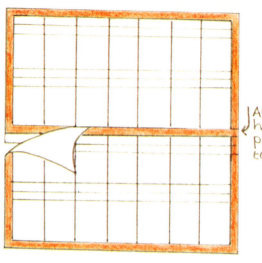

Attach here with paste or tape.

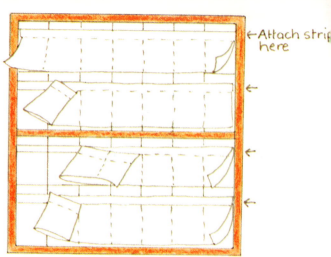

←Attach strip here

THIRD SUNDAY IN ADVENT	MONDAY	TUESDAY	WEDNESDAY
REJOICE	This week, make a Christmas crib.	*I will lead my blind people by roads they have never travelled. I will turn their darkness into light.* *Is 42*	Write down or draw three thir you hope for. T about your hop with a friend. 1. 2. 3.
FOURTH SUNDAY IN ADVENT	CHRISTMAS DAY		
HOPE	Today, enjoy the plum pudding while celebrating Christ's birth.		

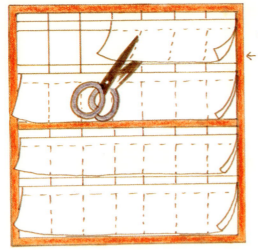

Cut off
← doors
like this

The day Christmas falls on varies each year.
You will need to change the last week of
your calendar each year.

THURSDAY	FRIDAY	SATURDAY
Sing heavens! Shout for joy, earth! The Lord will comfort his people. *Is 49*	Give a helping hand.	Think quietly for five minutes about the Christmas story.

The Christmas Story

What Will This Child Be?

When Herod was king, there lived in Judaea a priest called Zechariah. He and his wife Elizabeth were good people who followed the commandments faithfully. Elizabeth had never had a child and they were both getting old.

One day, Zechariah was alone offering sacrifice in the temple. An angel appeared to him and Zechariah was very afraid. The angel said to him: "Zechariah, do not be afraid. Your prayer has been heard. Your wife Elizabeth will have a son. You must call him John. He will be filled with the Holy Spirit. He will bring disobedient people back to good ways. He will prepare the people for the Lord who is coming."

Zechariah said: "How do I know whether this is true? My wife and I are both very old." The angel replied: "I am Gabriel who comes from the presence of God and I have been sent to speak to you and bring you this good news. Because you have not believed my words, which will come true at the proper time, you will be silent until these things I have told you have all happened."

When Zechariah came out of the temple he could not speak. "He must have seen a vision," people said.

Some time later, Elizabeth conceived a child. In the sixth month of her pregnancy an angel was sent by God to Nazareth in Galilee. The angel went to a maiden named Mary and said: "Mary, do not be afraid. You are to have a son and you must name him Jesus. He will be called Son of the Most High God. He will be a king as his ancestor David was, and his kingdom will never end." Mary said: "But how can this be? I am a virgin."

"The Holy Spirit will come to you and the power of God will be upon you," the angel answered. "For this reason the child will be called the Son of God. Your cousin Elizabeth, who is now old and was childless, is already carrying a child. Nothing is impossible with God."

"I am the handmaid of the Lord," said Mary. "Let what you have said happen." And the angel left her.

Mary travelled through the hill country to visit Elizabeth. As soon as Mary spoke, Elizabeth was filled with God's spirit and she knew Mary's secret. "Why should the mother of my Lord visit me?" she asked.

Mary was glad she could share her happiness. "God has remembered me and he has remembered his promises to our people. He is coming soon to help us."

When Elizabeth's baby was born the neighbors and relations came to share her joy. They thought the baby would be called Zechariah after his father, but Elizabeth spoke up. "He is to be called John." "But no one in your family has that name," people said. "What does Zechariah want?" And they turned to see. Zechariah took a writing tablet and wrote, "His name is John."

Immediately his speech returned and he began to praise God:

Let us praise the Lord, the God of Israel.
He promised through his prophets long ago
that he would save us from our enemies
and those who hate us,
so that we might serve him without fear
all the days of our life.
You, my child, will be called a prophet of the Most High God.
You will go ahead of the Lord to prepare his road for him.
Our God is merciful and tender.
He will cause the bright dawn of salvation to rise on us
and he will guide our steps in the path of peace.

The neighbors were all filled with fear. Everyone who heard the story thought about it and wondered, "What is this child going to be?"

John grew in body and spirit until the time he was a man. Then he went about preaching to people. "Turn away from your sins and be baptized and God will forgive you. It's time to get the way ready for the Lord who is coming soon."

Mary's Song

Words by WENDY POUSSARD

Music by CHRISTOPHER WILLCOCK

Brightly

1. I'm hap-py, I'm hap-py. My heart sings and dan-ces God
2. God came to a poor girl, Ma-ry of Gali-lee He
3. I'm hap-py, I'm hap-py. I sing my song of praise. God

1. fills us with his grace. He makes our home his dwelling place
2. chose her for his own, And in her his power was shown.
3. puts down migh-ty kings, Fills the hun-gry with good things.

1. I say yes to my God, His good news is his ans-wer.
2. I am not proud or fa-mous, But God does his work through me
3. He watches o-ver us And is with us all our days.

Refrain: God pro-mised he would care for us, He will al-ways be there for us. His

pro-mises come true. There is nothing our God cannot do. There is nothing our God cannot do.

Dove Communications Pty. Ltd.

Jesus Is Born

Emperor Augustus ordered a census to be taken through the Roman Empire. All the people went to their own towns to put their names on the roll. Joseph and Mary set out from the town of Nazareth in Galilee and travelled to Bethlehem in Judaea. Bethlehem had been the home town of the great King David. It was also Joseph's home town.

Mary was pregnant and while they were in Bethlehem the time came for her to have her baby. She gave birth to her first son, wrapped him up in swaddling clothes, which were like long strips of cloth, and laid him in an animals' feed box. He was born in a stable because there was no room for them at the inn.

There were some shepherds in the fields near the town. They lived in the open and took turns watching the sheep during the night. An angel of the Lord appeared to them and the glory of the Lord shone round them. They were very much afraid. But the angel said to them: "Don't be afraid. I bring you good news to share with all the people. Today, in the town of David, a savior has been born to you; he is Christ the Lord. This is how you will know him: you will find him wrapped in swaddling clothes and lying in a manger." Suddenly the shepherds saw a great crowd of angels praising God and singing:

Glory to God in the highest
And peace on earth to those who are
God's friends.

When the angels went away, the shepherds said to one another, "Let us go to Bethlehem to see this thing which the Lord has made known to us." They hurried away and found Mary and Joseph and saw the baby Jesus lying in the manger. When the shepherds saw the child they repeated what the angels had said about him. Everyone was astonished. And Mary treasured all these things and kept them in her heart.

The Wise Men Look for a King

Far away in the East lived some rich and powerful men, wise rulers in their own land. One night, they saw a strange star rising in the sky, a star whose name they did not know, for they had never seen it before.

These wise men had heard how the Jewish people hoped for a great king who would soon be born to save them, as Moses had saved their ancestors. When they saw the new star they tried to puzzle out its meaning. A new star! Perhaps it meant that the new king had come!

They decided to go at once and search for him. They chose rich gifts to take on their journey. Gold for a king. Incense for a God. A bitter perfume called myrrh for a leader who would suffer and die for his people.

The wise men followed the star to Jerusalem. There they visited Herod, the King of Judaea. Perhaps they thought they would find the new king in his rich palace. "Where is the baby who is born to be king of the Jews?" they asked. King Herod was shocked. He called together his high priests and advisors. "What's this I hear about a new king whose birth is foretold by our prophets? Where will he be born?" "At Bethlehem in Judaea," his advisors told him. "That is what the prophet wrote."

Herod met secretly with the wise men of the East. "Go and find out all about the child," he said, "and when you have found him, let me know so that I may visit him too." But Herod had made a cruel plan to kill the child. He did not want any new kings in *his* kingdom.

The wise men continued their long journey. To their delight they saw the new star again, moving above them in the night sky. They followed it to Bethlehem, and there they found the child with Mary, his mother. They opened their gifts and gave them to Jesus.

The wise men did not go back to Herod, for they were warned in a dream how dangerous this would be. Quietly they returned to their own country by a different way.

What do you think the wise men expected to find at the end of their journey?

How do you think they felt when they found Jesus?

What do you think of their gifts? What gift would you have given?

THE EPIPHANY
THE TWELFTH DAY OF CHRISTMAS

When the wise men came from the East, Mary showed Jesus, for the first time, to people from far away. This event is sometimes called the Epiphany. The name comes from a Greek word and it means *showing.* It reminds Christians that Jesus' life was important, not only for people of his own land, but for the whole world. The whole feast of Christmas is about "showing," because Jesus shows the world who God is. In Jesus, God and man are one.

The feast of the Epiphany was celebrated for many centuries on January 6, "The twelfth day of Christmas." Now some churches remember it on the Sunday closest to this date. On the feast of the Epiphany you may like to add the figures of the wise men to your Christmas crib. Some people take down the Christmas tree and decorations, because this day marks the end of the Christmas season.

Little One

Words by WENDY POUSSARD

Music by CHRISTOPHER WILLCOCK

Not too fast

1. Lit- tle one, so new, so small, You come to us with no- thing at all. You
2. Lit- tle one are you surprised By an an- gels song from mid- night skies? An
3. Lit- tle one, when you are grown Your blood will stain the cob- ble- stones. But your

1. have a feed- box for a bed And go to sleep in the a- ni-mal's shed. The
2. or- der came from dis- tant Rome, So you lie in a ci- ty far from home.
3. words will bring the mour- ners joy, Your peace will ne- ver be des- troyed.

1. rich and wise don't come inside. Poor shepherds share the secret that you hide.
2. Ma- ry and Jo-seph watch the snow And keep you warm, and wonder where to go.
3. Ma- ry sings a lulla- by And holds you in her arms so you won't cry.

slightly faster

Refrain: You are the brother of the tra- v'lling people, Your sa- ving journey has be- gun, To

bring your peace to a world that's broken, To bring your bread of life to the hun- gry ones.

Making a Crib

PAPER CRIB

Trace the shapes onto stiff paper or light cardboard

    The purple shapes are for Joseph.

    The blue shape is Mary.

    The orange shape is the baby.

    The brown shapes are the crib.

Draw faces on Mary, Joseph and the baby.

Color in their clothes and the crib.

Mary and the baby and Joseph's bottom half.
Fold each piece in a cone shape joining along the dotted line.

Tape the top section of Joseph onto the Joseph cone at the point marked.

The crib.
Cut the ends of the rectangle as marked and fold up as shown. Tape the end pieces in position as in the sketch.

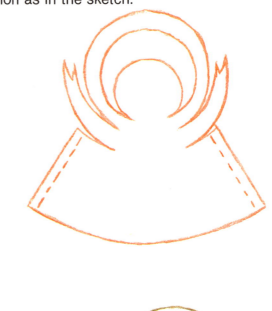

CUT 2

FOLD FOLD

A Light for Everyone

Words by WENDY POUSSARD

With steady movement

Music by CHRISTOPHER WILLCOCK

1. Stars were shi-ning in the night, Who knows how far a-way, When shepherds watching on the hills Ran
2. Wise men gazed in-to the skies. They saw a new star rise, And though they did not understand, They
3. Light a Christ-mas candle now, And light a Christmas star. O lit-tle child of Bethlehem, Light

1. down to Beth- le- hem to share The my- ste- ry of Christ- mas day.
2. fol-lowed where its promise led And found new ways of be- ing wise.
3. up our night by showing us The my- ste- ry of who you are.

Refrain: This child is born to us, This child is giv'n to us, A

shi- ning morning, A light for e- v'ry one, The light of all the na- tions dawn- ing.

Christmas Customs

Trudy Vaughan grew up in Germany. She still loves to remember the Christmases of her childhood. She says:

"In Germany, Christmas Eve is the time to give presents. We used to all gather in the living room around the Christmas tree. All the lights would be out and the big tree with lighted candles looked so beautiful. Outside the snow would be thick on the ground.

"All the presents would be ready around the tree and we'd sing Christmas carols — *O Tannenbaum* (that's *O Christmas Tree)* and *Silent Night.* Then we used to give each other presents and open them and show them to each other.

"We used to have special cookies to eat. My mother used to start baking them in November and she used recipes that she only used at Christmas time. She used to hide the cookies so we wouldn't eat them before Christmas came. We used to have Christmas cake too. It had raisins and nuts in it, but it was light colored, not dark like fruitcake. Of course, in those days we hardly ever had gifts and treats of cakes and cookies. The only time we were given gifts was at Christmas, so it was very, very special and exciting.

"Then we'd go to the neighbors' homes and they would show us their presents. We used to wait up for Midnight Mass and we'd all go. It was very, very cold. But the bells and carols and lights and the Mass were so beautiful, it was worth it.

"Christmas Day itself was our time for a reunion with all our relations. We'd have a special meal and meet somewhere with our uncles and aunts and cousins."

In England the Christmas Pudding is a special part of Christmas. The pudding often has a surprise in it, like a thimble or a coin.

People say that if you find a ring you'll be the first one married. If you find a thimble you'll be an old maid. If you find a button you'll be a bachelor. And if you find a coin you'll be rich someday.

In France lots of people stay up for Midnight Mass. Afterward they come home and eat Christmas Dinner. After dinner they often have a special dessert — chocolate cake frosted with whipped cream.

In Australia Christmas comes in summertime. It is the biggest festival of the year. Children have long school holidays after Christmas and lots of families go to the beach or to the country.

Christmas trees, gifts, decorations, carols and family get-togethers are all part of Christmas in the United States.

Have any of your friends lived in another land? Find out how Christmas is celebrated there. Do they have special Christmas decorations or customs from that country that they still use?

The Shell Necklace

Cathy gazed at the necklace. It was made of rows of shells, closely strung together so that the shape of each shell fitted into the next and the whole effect was of a rippling chain. The smooth, glassy surface of each shell was a creamy color, with deeper touches of gold. When she held the necklace in her hands she could dream about where the shells had come from; deep tropical seas, warm golden beaches, and dark people who talked and laughed with their friends while their fingers cleverly threaded the shells.

Now the necklace lay in Elaine's drawer with some earrings and other jewelry. And Cathy was admiring it as she often did.

Elaine and Cathy were cousins. Elaine was 18, nearly 10 years older than Cathy, but they had always been good friends. Cathy loved to spend hours in Elaine's room, listening to stories about her work and her friends, and admiring her clothes and jewelry. But the shell necklace was her favorite. It was much more beautiful than anything Cathy had ever seen. She thought Elaine was the luckiest person on earth to own such a thing.

"Please, Elaine, tell me about the necklace," Cathy said.

And this is the story Elaine told her.

"The necklace comes from the Caribbean. My family went there once for a vacation. I loved the beaches, the trees and ferns, the gardens and fruit, the tall sharp mountains and the dark people who were so friendly and kind. We stayed with my parents' friends in a city, where there are modern buildings and roads and enormous lawns and gardens.

"One day our host Bill said: 'I'm going to Loa's house to see his new refrigerator. Come with me and you will see the kind of house the local people live in.'

"Loa worked as a gardener. He was very proud of his house because it was built the way the Europeans build houses, of wood and iron, not palm and bamboo. Outside the house was a neat garden. There were many fruits and vegetables growing, and also flowers.

"I went inside. It was the smallest house I had ever seen. It was really just one (not

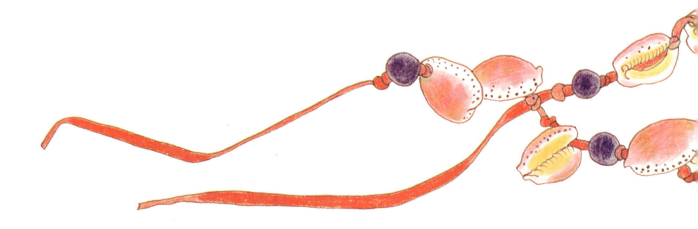

very large) room. In one corner there was an area screened off for sleeping. There was a tiny stove, no sink or cupboards, a table but no chairs. On the walls there were some pictures from a magazine carefully cut out and pasted up to make the room prettier.

"I felt uncomfortable and rather shocked. I had never been in a house that had so few possessions. I kept comparing it with my own house (which suddenly seemed absolutely enormous) with its carpets, curtains, TV set, machines of all sorts, books, records and other possessions. I could see that these people owned almost nothing. The 'new' refrigerator stood in a corner, but I had never seen a refrigerator as old or as little before.

"I wasn't used to standing up inside a house, but if there are no chairs, that is what you must do, or else sit on the floor. Then I realized that Loa and his wife and daughter were very, very proud of this house. I had never felt as proud of my house as this family was.

"They spoke to me gently and their little daughter watched with big eyes and occasionally came over to me and touched my arms and my dress and made admiring noises. That was the other uncomfortable bit. I realized how proud the family was to have *me* in their house. I felt like a famous person. I had never been made to feel so special and so welcome in my life.

"Then the little girl whispered to her mother and ran into the bedroom. She returned with a beautiful shell necklace in her hands and gave it to me.

"I waited a long time. Then I put out my hand and took the gift."

Elaine picked up the shells and ran them through her fingers. She held them up to the window, the sun shone on the pearly surfaces and made them gleam. Then she handed the necklace to Cathy. "I thought these would look beautiful with your new dress at Christmas time. Keep them for a while and while you still love them, give them away. And be sure to tell the story."

What did the Caribbean family teach Elaine about gifts?
Tell a story you know of a special gift.
  OR
Draw a picture of the gift.

St. Nicholas' Story

My name is Nicholas — Saint Nicholas — Santa Claus for short. In the third century I lived on earth. I was a bishop then, in the city of Myra. Books say that very little is known of me. You have heard rumors, perhaps, about my gifts and miracles. There is some truth in those stories, but they took place so long ago that I cannot be too exact about them myself. After my death, I was declared a saint, and saints, I think, should not exaggerate.

I am astonished to see how I have been remembered! How I have been loved! People call me Santa Claus or Father Christmas. They tell amazing tales of how I go down chimneys and drive through the sky in a sleigh pulled by reindeer. I am honored by all this attention, though some of the stories make me laugh. When children say, "I do not believe in Santa Claus," I feel just a little sad.

The Tree's Story

I grow in The-Forest-Of-The-World. In the snows of winter, I am green. In the dry brown heat of summer, I am still green. A man sings a song beneath my shady branches. He is old, but not as old as I. I am the oldest living thing in all the world.

When it is Christmas time in The-Forest-Of-The-World, children and parents cut off my lowest branches and take them into their houses. Then their homes smell like the forest. The children cover the branches with shining tinsel and stars. They remember the birth of a child they call the Son of Man.

He was like a tree, they say, growing tall by the waterside. He was like a vine in his

father's garden. His kingdom was like a tiny seed that grew into a tree where birds could build their nests. He was a carpenter, this Christmas Man, and he died when he was young on a wooden cross.

The people in the houses put gifts beneath my branches. The Son of Man has given himself to us, they say. We will give to each other.

After Christmas my branches are taken out of the houses and thrown away. But I live on. Another winter, another summer. I grow. I reach into the sky. Next Christmas the people will come to me again.

What Do Gifts Say?

During Advent we prepare gifts for our family, friends and neighbors. We give gifts to remind us of the gift that God sent us at the first Christmas — his own son to share our human life. What do our gifts say?

1st Reader   *Placing a gift he has made near the crib.*

My gift says, "Thank you." Thank you for your friendship, your companionship, your love. Thank you for the talking we do, the games we've played together, the times you've helped me.

All   Thank you Heavenly Father for our family, friends and neighbors.

2nd Reader   *Placing the gift of an apple near the crib.*

My gift says, "I'm sorry." I'm sorry for all the times I've been unkind, when I wouldn't help, when I've said angry words to hurt you. Can you see I want to make it up? Have you noticed me trying?

All   We are sorry Heavenly Father for the times we have broken your law of love. We have hurt the ones you gave us to love.

3rd Reader   *Placing the gift of a flower near the crib.*

My gift says, "Please." Please stay and be my friend. I want to share my life with you even more.

All   Heavenly Father, share your gift of life with us. Teach us to be open to your gifts and your love.

4th Reader   *Placing the gift of a lighted candle near the crib.*

All   My gift says, "Love." I love you. Thank you for loving me. From you I learn what God's love is.

Heavenly Father, thank you for your love. Thank you for sending your son, Jesus Christ, so we can see your love in a human person. Thank you for showing your love in all the people I love, and all the people who love me.

The Travelling People

If Jesus were born this Christmas, who are the travelling people he would be born among?

Would it be a family whose home has been destroyed by disasters of floods or earthquakes? There are many of these families today.

Would it be a family that has had to escape from war, leaving any possessions behind, and arriving without a job or shelter in a strange land? That is happening to many families right now.

There are families that live in a rich country, but don't share in the riches or the well-being. Maybe a member of the family is sick, or the father cannot get a job, or the family is being destroyed by drugs or alcohol or mental illness. Jesus could be born among these people.

Would it be a family that struggles to pay its bills, to do all its tasks, to care for one another, and to share and care for others outside the family too?

Would it be a family like your family?

At Christmas time Christians remember their brothers who are struggling with difficulties. Most groups of Christians join together to give to those in need. We don't give only to our families or to those who love us. We give something that counts to someone who really needs it.

What are you and your friends preparing to give to today's travelling people?

Gifts for Christmas

Here are some Christmas gifts you can make for your friends or family.

SOME GIFTS TO EAT

PEANUT BUTTER CREAMS

Ingredients ¼ cup powdered sugar
1 cup chocolate chips
½ cup sweetened
condensed milk
1 cup peanut butter

Method Put the ingredients into a bowl in the order listed.

Stir.

Drop by spoonfuls onto waxed paper on a cookie sheet.

Or roll into balls ½″ in diameter.

Chill until firm.

Gifts for Christmas

SHORTBREAD

Ingredients 1½ cups flour
4 tablespoons cornstarch
¼ cup sugar
1 cup (2 sticks) butter

Method   Sift flour and cornstarch. Add sugar and butter and work into a stiff dough.

Turn onto a lightly floured board and knead well.

Divide dough into three equal portions.

Roll or pat each portion into a round ¼" to ⅜" thick.

Cut each round into eight segments, prick and carefully lift onto a cookie sheet.

Bake in a slow oven 325° F 15-20 minutes.

Cool on a rack.

COOKIES

Use Christmas cookie cutters to make cookies in the shapes of stars, Christmas trees, candles and angels. You can use your favorite sugar cookie recipe or a packaged cookie mix.

Sprinkle cookies with colored sugar to make them prettier.

Gifts for Christmas

SOME GIFTS TO MAKE

POMANDERS

Ingredients (for each pomander)

      1 small smooth-skinned orange
      1 oz. whole cloves
      A length of velvet ribbon
      A piece of thin wire.

Method   Press the cloves right into the orange. (This needs to be done carefully or the skin of the orange will split and spoil the shape of the pomander.)

Fold the wire in half and push the two ends straight through the center of the orange. Leave a loop at the top on which to fasten the ribbon and fold the remainder of the wire around the orange.

Hang the clove-studded oranges in a cool, airy place until dry (from 2 - 6 weeks). They are then ready to perfume a drawer, a suitcase or a closet.

Crab apples may be used in place of the oranges. Fewer cloves are required and the pomander takes less time to complete.

Gifts for Christmas

DECORATED CANDLES

You will need plain white candles, carving tools, felt-tipped pens, poster paints, brushes, colored paper and ribbons.

Decorate the candle by drawing and painting on it with the felt-tipped pens or poster paints.

If you want a carved design on your candle, draw it first with pencil. Gently scratch the design into the wax, gradually cutting as deep as you want to go. Make sure the candle is resting on a smooth surface as you work so it won't break.

Now use the felt-tipped pens or the poster paints to color the design on your candle.

Fold and cut colored paper to make a candleholder,   OR
tie a ribbon around the candle.

CANDLESTICKS

You will need some clay, some seeds — dried peas, lentils, pumpkin seeds or other fairly big, sharp seeds. You can buy seeds at health food stores.

Knead the clay till it is smooth. Shape it into either a cone or a flattened ball.

Make a depression in the top to hold a candle.

Now start making a design on the candlestick by pressing in the seeds. If you choose sharp, pointy seeds and press the sharp end into the clay, they will stick better.

Spray or paint the candlestick with lacquer as soon as you have finished. Leave the bottom and the depression for the candle unlacquered so the clay can dry.

Gifts for Christmas

DRIED FLOWERS IN A STAND

This is similar to the candlestick idea.

Make a little "vase" out of clay. Leave it solid — no hollow center.

Decorate the outside by pressing a pattern into the clay using your fingernail or some other hard object such as a knife, seed or small bottle top.

Use a skewer to make three holes in the "vase" to hold the dried flowers.

When the clay dries arrange tiny seed heads, dried flowers and leaves in it.

You can make an incense holder in the same way.

SEEDS, SEEDPODS AND DRIED GRASSES

These can be used to make:

Necklaces: String seeds or shells together. They can be painted with gold, silver or bronze paint.

Christmas tree decorations: String large, unusually shaped seeds together. Spray paint them with gold or silver paint.

Try arranging grasses or seed heads to make stars.

Gifts for Christmas

MAKING CHRISTMAS CARDS

Try cutting Christmas shapes out of
construction paper or cardboard.

The drawings show how to make a card in
a Christmas tree, a candle or an angel
shape. Decorate the card by pasting on
colored paper in a design, or using felt-
tipped pen or crayon.

Write a special Christmas greeting. Here
are some ideas:

Love was born at Christmas.
Christ is born in peaceful men.
At Christmas we remember when God
came and walked among men.
Good news to all men.
Peace upon earth.

The next pictures show how you can make
a Christmas scene on a card and fold it so
it will stand up.

Scraps of material and colored paper
make very rich, colorful cards.

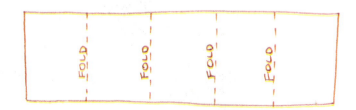

We Remember

Words by WENDY POUSSARD AND MOIRA EASTMAN

Music by CHRISTOPHER WILLCOCK

At a gentle pace

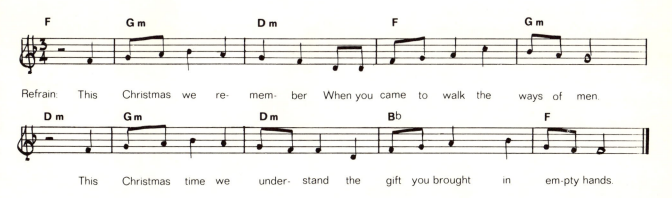

Refrain: This Christmas we re-mem-ber When you came to walk the ways of men.

This Christmas time we under-stand the gift you brought in em-pty hands.

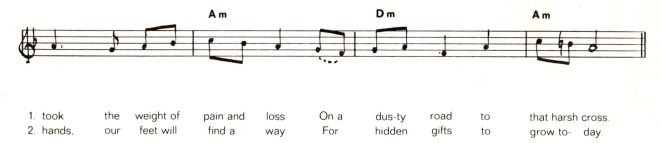

1. You travelled with us on sandalled feet through winter cold and summer heat. You
2. You touched us gen-tly with healing hands. You taught our feet the way to dance, Our

1. took the weight of pain and loss On a dus-ty road to that harsh cross.
2. hands, our feet will find a way For hidden gifts to grow to-day.

Repeat Refrain.

Acknowledgments

To Eva Adams, Alan Baxter, Pat Campitelli,
Heather Cumming, Ann Guiney, Vianney Hatton,
Shirley Macdonald, Jenni Mitchell and
Mark Zitterschlager who have contributed
their knowledge, encouragement and criticism
to this project.

Paper cut-out crib, pp. 24-25, Judith Leahy

Photography, Michael Coyne

Nihil Obstat:

    Gerard Diamond
    Diocesan Censor

Imprimatur:

    Peter J. Connors, D.C.L.
    Vicar General

    Date: June, 1978

Library of Congress Catalog Card Number: 80-68368

International Standard Book Number: 0-87793-214-x

Printed and bound in the United States of America